Contents

How to play your kalimba
STANDARD 10-NOTE KALIMBA IN C SCALE

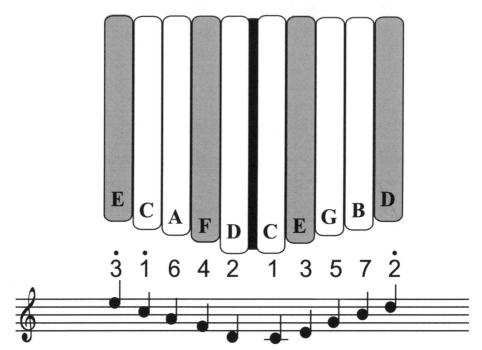

On most 8-10-tine kalimbas, the center tine will be a C note.

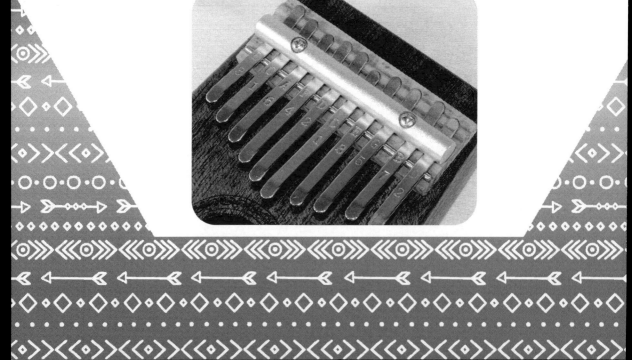

STANDARD 17-NOTE KALIMBA IN C SCALE

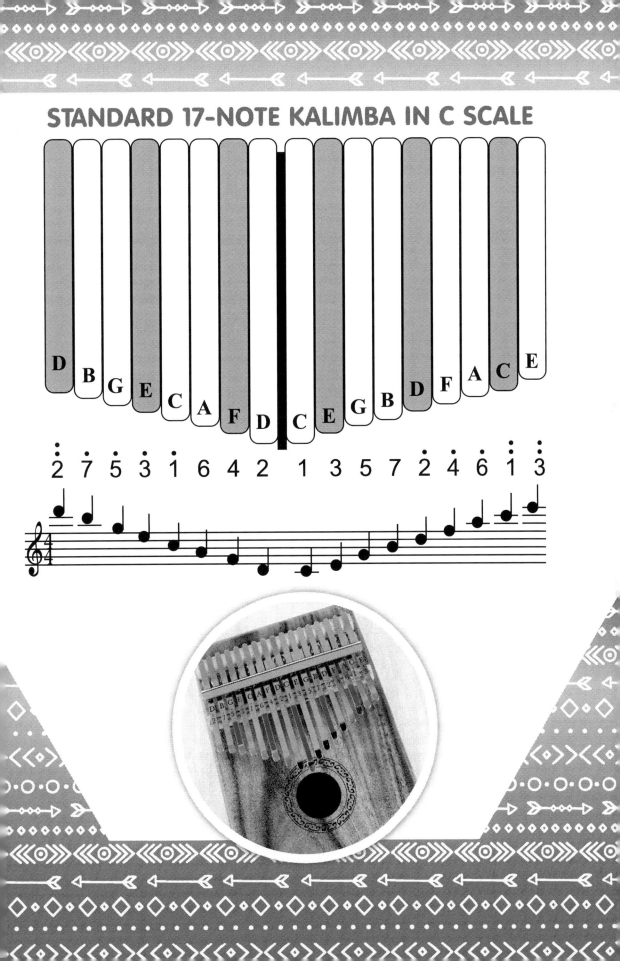

HOW TO HOLD AND PLAY YOUR KALIMBA

- Hold the kalimba with your your thumb on the keys and your other fingers on the side.
- Using your nails to strike the keys will minimize finger pain and make the sound more crisp.
- Use your middle finger to cover the hole on the back to create a WAH sound.
- Train your thumb to move easily between all the keys on each side.

Our sheet music is universal and suitable for 8-17 note kalimbas.

Each of the modern kalimbas usually has enlarged numbers and letters representing the name of the notes. The standard 17 Note Kalimba contains 3 octaves:
1) a full 2nd small octave,
2) a 3rd small octave, and
3) 3 notes from the 4th small octave.

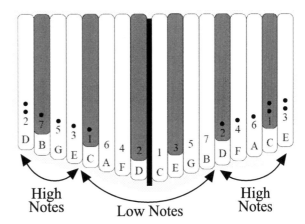

High Notes   Low Notes   High Notes

The 2nd small octave goes from C4 to C5 and is depicted in our sheet music as simple numbers. The notes from the 3rd small octave have numbers with one dot above each number. The 3 notes from the 4th small octave - C6, D6, and E6 - are depicted by numbers with two dots above them.

Follow the numbers… and begin to play!
This book might include only numbers and it will be enough to begin to play, but we decided to add classic note symbols to help teach them and show musical notation.

Attention: Songs have been transposed for a DIATONIC range. Some melodies might be changed and simplified.

We add a QRcode to all songs. Follow the link and listen to the rhythm before beginning to play.

Music is an integral part of the life of Native Americans, playing a key role in ceremonies, recreational activities, self-expression, and healing. Many different instruments are used in Native American music, including drums, flutes, and other percussion instruments. The human voice is possibly the most important element of their music. Singing accompanied by drumming is used by Native Americans in a variety of musical genres, including lullabies, spiritual songs and healing chants. Music accompanies daily activities, particularly during religious ceremonies, work, games, courtship, hunting, farming, war and storytelling.

Native American tribes include music with melodies which are both secular and sacred. Secular music can be used in songs to honor a person's life or to express gratitude in communal celebrations. Sacred music is played when addressing spiritual issues, the afterlife or the Earth's elements. Overall, however, Native Americans perceive the link between the sacred and secular and don't distinguish between the two.

Lyrics in many Native American songs are simple vocables which are non-lexical or nonsensical, and most commonly mark the beginning and end of phrases, sections or other elements of a song. Most Navajo songs, for example, are non-translatable and lack a clear or evident meaning. Syllable choice often depends on the song's mood. Traditional Indigenous American songs usually begin with a slow and steady beat and then grow gradually faster and more emphatic. Percussion, such as drums (including the water wooden tongue drum) and different kinds of rattles, usually a gourd with seeds, seashells, or stones inside, are common and a very important accompaniment to the music. It is also common to use instruments which mimic sounds from nature, such as the rainstick and ocean drum.

Native Americans have never known the thumb piano. The kalimba came from Africa but it is perfectly suitable for any tribal songs.

The most difficult thing about playing Native American songs is their irregular rhythms. It might change several times during a song because rhythm is generally more important than melody. Songs for American tribes are traditionally a method of communicating with their ancestors and supernatural powers. Music is used to help grow a harvest, bring rain, bring victory in battle or cure the sick.

Music is seldom performed for its own sake and as a rule, the tribes tried to repeat sounds which were heard in nature (whispering winds, rain sounds, etc). That is why the rhythm prevailed and words were not so important. Some songs such as ceremonial or medicinal ones often were inspired by dreams. Here you can find traditional songs, handed down from generation to generation: ceremonial (such as corn grinding or moccasin game songs) and a medicinal song.

Ani Couni Chaouani

Arapaho Song

Version 1

Ani Couni Chaouani

Arapaho Song
Version 2

Ani Couni Chaouani

Arapaho Song

Version 3

Medicine Song

Apache Song

Bebi Notsa

Creek Lullaby

Be - bi no - tsa, no - tsa,

no - tsa, lut - sa ho - po kan, ai - yang - si

buk - sin no thla thla ga his ma - ki - to

ai - yang - si Be - bi no - tsa

Buffalo Dance

Kiowa folk song

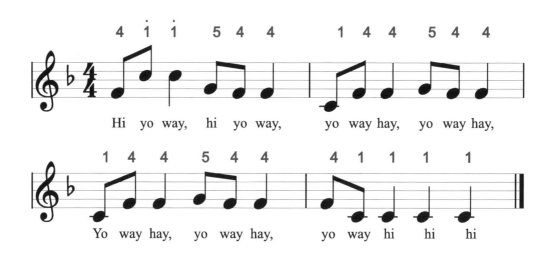

Chippewa Lullaby

Chippewa folk song

Corn Grinding Song

Zuni folk song

Dust of the Red Wagon

Ute folk song

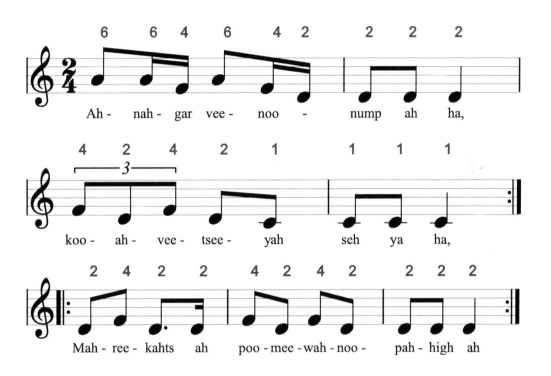

Eagle Dance Song

Algonquin folk song

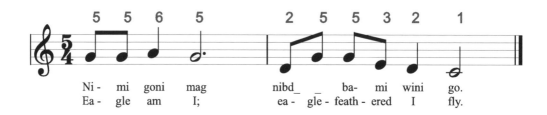

Ni - mi goni mag   nibd_ _ ba - mi wini go.
Ea - gle am I;   ea - gle - feath - ered I fly.

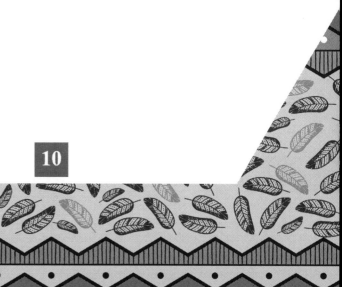

Epanay

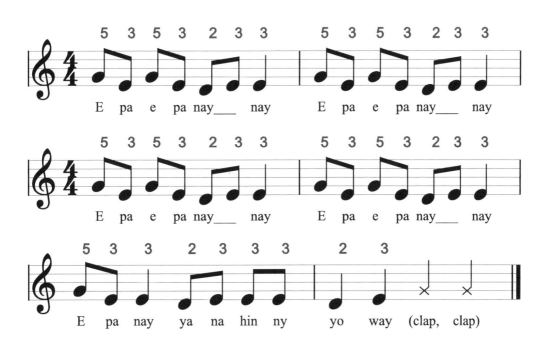

Eskimo Ice Cream

Inuit folk song

Yu rah ah rayk kum kun ong ah eh vay kum kun Yu

rah ah rayk kum kun_____ ong ah eh vay kum kun

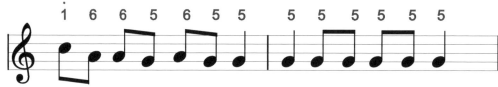

I - eye yuk who aye yah hah I yuk who aye yah hah

Yahk hah hye eye yah Yu yah

Hiya Hiya

Pawnee folk song

Happy Song

Navajo folk song

Ho Ho Watanay

Iroquois Lullaby
Version 1

Version 2

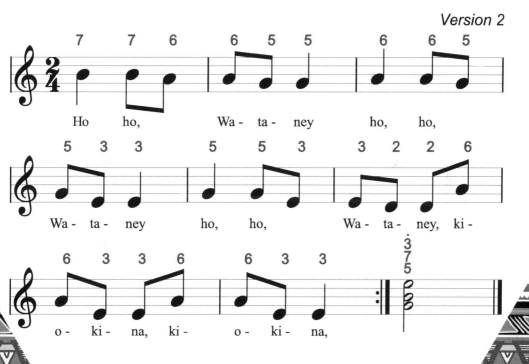

Hosisipa

Sioux folk song

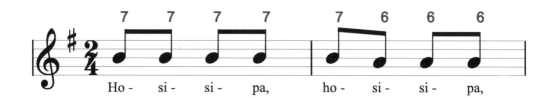

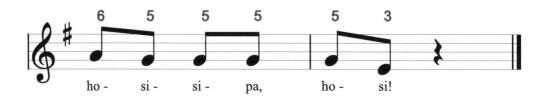

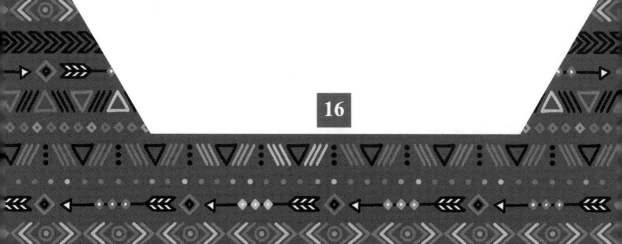

Hwi ne ya he

Presumably an Apache song

Happiness Song

Navajo folk song

Inuit Lullaby

Inuit folk song

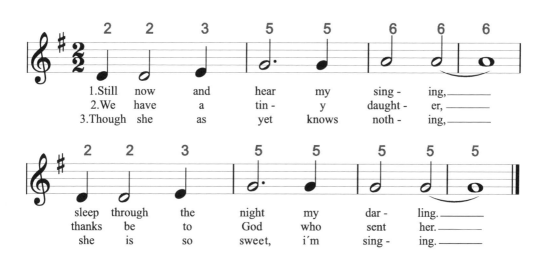

	2	2	3	5	5	6	6	6
1.Still	now	and	hear	my	sing -	ing,		
2.We	have	a	tin -	y	daught -	er,		
3.Though	she	as	yet	knows	noth -	ing,		

	2	2	3	5	5	5	5	5
sleep	through	the	night	my	dar -	ling.		
thanks	be	to	God	who	sent	her.		
she	is	so	sweet,	i'm	sing -	ing.		

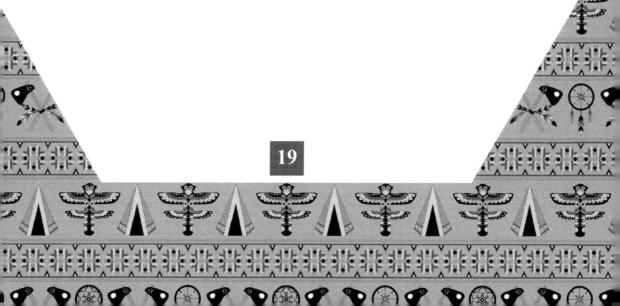

Moccasin Game Song

Navajo folk song

Nessa, Nessa

Ojibwe Lullaby

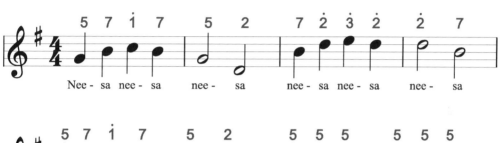

Mos Mos

Hopi folk song

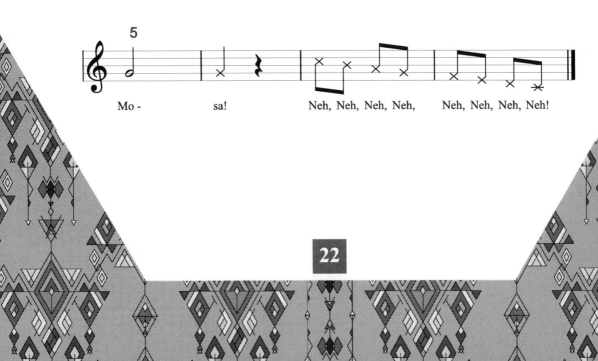

My Paddle*

Folk Song

* This is not an authentic Native American song but it captures the native spirit.

23

O Hal'lwe

Nanticoke folk song

Okki Tokki Unga

Eskimo fishing song

Sioux Lullaby

Sioux folk song

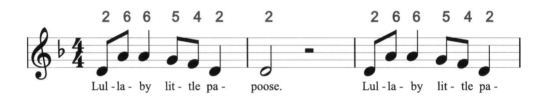

Wanagi Wacipi Olowan

Dakota folk song

He,   he,_   _ wan - na   wa - wa - te,

He,   he,_   _ wan - na   wa - wa - te,

Wa - na   wa - tin - ke,   Wa - na   wa - tin - ke.

Wioste Olowan

Dakota folk song

We N' De Ya Ho

Cherokee Morning Song

Zuni Sunset Song

Zuni folk song

Made in the USA
Middletown, DE
17 April 2021